C/45

GW01080176

Dreaming of Walls Repeating Themselves

Pat Winslow

Templar Poetry

First Published 2007 by Templar Poetry
Templar Poetry is an imprint of Delamide & Bell

Fenelon House,
Kingsbridge Terrace
Dale Road, Matlock, Derbyshire
DE4 3NB

www.templarpoetry.co.uk

ISBN 978-1-906285-03-6

Typeset by Pliny
Graphics by Paloma Violet
Printed and bound in India

To Steph

Acknowledgements

Carterton Pride: Tin Shacks to Beacon Town (ITHACA)
A Local Heritage Initiative Project commission - *His Photos*
The Interpreter's House - *Imagine* - *Mycroft and Sherlock*
Stand - *Dreaming of Walls Repeating Themselves* - *His Photos*
Poems 27 (Lancaster Litfest) - *Blyton*
Poetry Nottingham - *A Different Kind of Minute*
Vision On (Ver Poets) - *Zero*

Contents

A Different Kind of Minute

There's a different kind of minute
where time goes backwards,

where diamonds re-enter rocks,
and factories suck back their waste.

A baby might return to its womb
and a mother might climb down from the tree.

Floods will recede and clouds drink rain,
a dead boy will breathe in his father's arms again.

Missiles will leave a hospital.
Legless children will step back from mines.

Arms deal signatures will unwrite themselves
and ink travel back up inside the pen.

In time a fist could become a hand again.

Serial

1. Hands

His hands are in his lap. He won't write.
He won't even pick up the pencil.
Sometimes, he doesn't eat.

His arms refuse to move. He'll
sit for days, watching the sun's slow
forensic sweep across his cell.

The past is more real now:
a ribbon round his daughter's calliper
looped into a jaunty bow.

At night he sings to her.
He makes shadow dogs leap and yap.
He likes to stand behind and brush her hair.

Sometimes he just picks the mail up from the mat
or fixes things that might need mending.
Mostly, though, his hands just lie in his lap.

2. Black and White

She meant to split her sister's heart like a plum.
Rage runs through her like a magenta seam.

She's seen it in others, hot and inexplicable.
She could have ended up like that barmy girl

with the knitted jumper and cherry lips.
She knows where her mother's scissors are kept.

She watches her hand lifting again and again
like that man behind the shower curtain.

She keeps seeing herself on the wall.
A Javanese puppet. Wayang Kulit, it's called.

She imagines herself in the papers, on the News,
her mother phoning Whitehall 1212.

3. The Lieutenant Colonel

It starts with animals. His wife's kitten,
shaved, poisoned and shut in the oven.
It ends with him having a starving man

held down, his right hand chopped off
for stealing. Then come hangovers, a cough
that won't go away. And it's not enough

that his daughter comes to see him or that
the other one writes, because it's his gut
that worries him, that and the fact his shit

is bright red. He can't stand, can't walk,
can't do anything these days but smoke,
unscrew another whiskey bottle and talk.

Two dead brothers, a rotten father. His fist
was all he had. And a gun. He was the first
to sign up and leave. Somehow, he kissed

my mother, or she kissed him. Anyhow,
I'm here and he's dead and I know
I have a half sister somewhere now.

He had another go at getting it right
but, war being what it is, he got out,
left them hoping like my mother hoped.

All he ever knew was loss,
which doesn't excuse
the knife and bullet, of course.

Hammond's Big Mistake

Saturday. The Guardian crossword and a pot of tea.
The grill hissed. The toast was doing nicely.

Then Hammond arrived, hopping from foot to foot,
with his children in descending height order.

Their milky eyes were swimming. His flicked about.
She's had her period, he kept saying. Flick, flick.

She'd gone full-term and he'd not known.
It was a trick, she said later. To see if he'd notice.

He noticed alright. Back from Tescos with the kids
and seven bags of shopping to find her screaming

on the floor with the telly on and her waters broken.
She had it in the ambulance. Next day she brought it home.

The same milk-blue eyes, the same pale skin.
But it wasn't his. You could tell it never would be.

The Front Room Picture

Sometimes, on Sunday evenings, after cups of tea and
                                        beetroot salad
and the Dickens serial on TV, the dust would blow in
                                        something fierce.

The well blades would start to turn. The barn door creaked
                                        and slammed.
There'd be horse sweat and coffee. Boot spurs clanked,
                                        holsters gleamed.

The knack of flinging a lasso so you could tether and tame
                                        in one move
was like whistling or learning to ride a bike. One day, it just
                                        happened.

Hard to see with the sun setting like that. Hard to tell
                                        where shadows ended
and the room began, unless they had toffees, or a cat sat in
                                        your lap,

or someone needed their feet rubbing. Then it was grime
                                        and soot
and a gas fire popping and someone with a pile of ironing to
                                        do.

Repertoire

It was hoovering up a cheese sandwich in one go
with her piano lid mouth. No bits on the carpet.
There was just the crust left in her hands. Neat.

And 10p pieces, one up each nostril so her nose
looked like one of those coin trays you see
on washing machines at the launderette.

Or walking on her hands whilst in the lotus position,
her elbows jammed against her knees.
A Buddha with chicken feet rocking side to side.

She could hurl a gob two metres away from her.
She could bite her lip and dig her nails in so hard
both hands would bleed. Her own stigmata.

No point asking. She'd never tell you.
She could keep a secret. Right to the end.
She could die and never tell you anything.

Dreaming of Walls Repeating Themselves

Years can pass in a night. This dream is a film of our lives,
how boots marched constantly beneath our windows,
how we couldn't go out for fear of what might happen.

It must be before dawn when one of them, a blond boy,
scales our wall and shoves his head through the window.
He aims his rifle into our terrified silence.

Out of the birdless grey they come, storming our stairs,
turning our apartments into barracks. We wait.
We know what happens next. It's happened before.

They line us up, choosing the strongest or the tallest.
It's a game. In the end, we all go, our bodies jammed
inside trucks that rattle through the dusty streets.

This being a film, I escape and live and wake remembering
every newsreel I've ever seen. There are blackbirds
singing in the trees outside. It isn't light here yet.

We watch TV. In Abu Dis, day is vivid and fully formed.
The graffiti is fresh. A soldier aims a rifle at a boy.
The people look the same to me. They always do.

Mycroft and Sherlock

You'd call them singular, I suppose.
They were forever counting.

How many steps from our bedpost to the tallboy,
how many stairs to the landing.

There wasn't a cupboard
they hadn't opened or found the key to.

They made an inventory
of everything from saucers to coats.

Holidays were a nightmare -
how many quarter-mile posts between stations,

what size boots the ticket inspector wore,
what he'd eaten the day before.

They could look at a train and tell you
what the weather was like in Carlisle.

You can't imagine how many friends we lost.
The 'samples' nurse found beneath their beds -

cigar butts, half-drained glasses, combs,
handkerchiefs and socks and underwear.

The drugs I can understand. Their father did it.
And at least it kept them quiet.

But the tendency to want the truth,
the whole truth and nothing but.

Our guests were MPs and businessmen.
Besides, I had a lover.

That was soon over. And my marriage.
They didn't care. They had each other.

And later, Sherlock had that doctor.
The signs were there, of course.

I just never saw them.

The Persistence of Memory

A man may dream of a son.
A man may dream of him
long after he's gone.

A man may sit on a chair
that is screwed to the ground
and stare quietly at the floor.

His past will bloom like a bruise.
Passports, books and letters,
the family suitcase full of photos.

His mother's in the kitchen flipping
chapatis from hand to hand. He thinks
of Dali's timeless clocks dripping

like hammered moons of bread
across her fingers. Beneath the tawa,
is the gas flame's uneven spread.

The house smells of jeera and lamb.
His sister keeps laughing in the hall.
His brother stands behind him.

The phone rings. Grief is coming
like the slow seep of an electrical fault
behind walls, an old flex burning.

Too hot, too dangerous to touch.
Do it! First his mother, now his brother.
Proof is final. What follows is the switch,

the absence of light, pressure, bone on bone,
his sister's neck, the things the papers said
he'd done, the silence and the unborn son.

Notes from a Prison Chapel

Sometimes when I'm waiting, the silence
reminds me of when I was thirteen.
Sunlight, holy water and incense,
a dozen veils in a cardboard box,
a candle flame in a small red glass.

Pray that the light doesn't go out.
It would mean the end of everything.
I prayed - but it never did - I talked
and ate sweets, I laughed at damnation.
Endless flames were hard to imagine.

Outside, is a group of prisoners
who can walk on water - the lino
shines brilliantly in these corridors.
They're grinning, tripping over laces.
They could be kids but for their voices.

Football fans, then. Sons with their dads
out for a pint before the match starts.
A group of workmates, a gang of lads.
How many? Numbers are important.
in this Home Office establishment.

Say twelve. You won't easily forget
good men and true, steps to recovery,
the keys on a phone, bars on a gate,
noon and midnight, stamps for your letters,
the days of Christmas, the months, the years.

Absence

She missed it. Perhaps they all missed it.
Visual grief. How white piled on white,
the grey impressions their footfalls made,
the clouds of breath as they hauled the wood
up the hill, the uneven tracks behind them.
They worked all morning to that rhythm.

The sky was almost cornflower but she
never said and I'm sure she didn't see
the ragged cuff as he removed his glove
to give the kindling one last shove
before he lit it. This wasn't the moment.
What followed was more important.

The silence before he struck the match,
the slight rattle of the box, the scratch
before the spark caught, how suddenly
a far off thrush sang like it was already
spring. The notes were hard and clear
like chips of ice, diamonds in the air.

He blew softly on the twigs and leaves.
A boy's first whistle. He got on his knees.
There was a faint click, a falling away.
Sound, again. So much was heard that day.
So many things weren't said. No one prayed.
The diaries went up and no one cried.

A box of jumpers. The wool smelt lonely.
She wouldn't forget that. The only
thing that didn't burn was the watch.
She found the tiny cogs in the wreckage
when she went back. She saw it then,
how time is nothing once it's gone.

Toads

Normally I'd laugh at three shuffling cowpats.
But the family who invaded our tent was terrified.

That morning, in flailing panic, they leapt
from bag to bag and took cover under clothes.

They disappeared beneath the groundsheet
and lost a baby in the grass.

There was something about their skin,
the thinness, that made me think of how

a hospital sounds at three a.m.,
the shim of steel, how we're cut open

and stitched up again, how we grow old
and our hair turns to cobwebs.

There was something about their fallibility
that made me know myself better,

and now, when I turn over in the night
and my weight drags across my bones,

I feel the girth of me sag and stretch a little more.
It never was alien skin. Not quite.

Blyton

She never told me, but I knew the salty smell of their boat.
I saw the oil spill by the mooring post, heard the engine,
felt the sway each time they set out, the tugging waves.

I could open a can of Carnation milk. I could fit a key
to a tin of sardines and roll back the lid, build fires,
read maps. I knew which way was true north.

Mostly, I knew how it would feel to be a flop-haired boy
who had string and a pen-knife and a torch in his pocket,
how sand stays in shoes long after the holidays are over.

Floored

You slide on the lino in your puffball nappy.
Fat arms and legs scuttle you into dark corners,
under tables and chairs whilst the adults talk.

And now is the first time you draw limbs
coming out of a body and not a head.

You have a tendency to fall over. Boys tie hankies
round your knees, plasters keep peeling off.
Runs like a crab they say in your report. Lollops.

Somehow you never learn to climb the ropes,
though you're always jumping off swings

and eating mouthfuls of earth. A crash landing
into a sink wrecks your teeth. Later it's bicycles,
a hole in the road, a bus coming up behind you,

the driver looking the wrong way. You learn
to hop to the loo. You wash standing on one leg,

start to walk again, this time the right way,
feet aligned perfectly below the knees. The shift
of balance is from fearless to hesitant. Water

hammocks you on Wednesdays after work.
Diving is the perfect fall. You do it well. Recovering.

The deep end doesn't scare you any more. Loss
is absence and absence is something new to learn.
So, here you are, walking dogs in middle age

in the soaking rain. If it means a wheelchair,
then let the tyres be slick and let there be gears.

And if it's cancer, let it be quick and still something
to write about. Just lately the ground is getting harder.
Maybe it's time someone else did all the work.

But you can't resist the odd spadeful, the thunk of it
hitting roots and stones. When the sun's above you

and the wind's baffling the grass, you can think
of no better place to be. All that damp stuff rotting down,
all that evidence shifting and settling, sifting into infinity.

Zero

The cleverest wound is the one that makes
a woman look down when someone speaks.

See the narrowing of her shoulders,
how she hesitates before opening doors.

A knife would have been quicker. Her face,
perhaps, might have seemed an easier price.

He'd have slit her neatly from mouth to ear,
cleaned her up and told her that he loved her.

Before and after. She'd have had that.
Not this white chain dragging day and night,

this frozen bell of disbelief that keeps
tolling in her head so hard she never sleeps.

When did it start? She has no memory.
She walks behind, watching his shadow sway.

First one foot, then the other. Such control
keeping up, being his little dead doll.

His Photos

Runways, planes, jeeps and parade grounds,
an overturned wagon with jagged metal sides,
three men standing around in the mud.

He was obsessed with repetition - a fat tyre tread,
bolts, rivets, boots, the day to day of Company B,
the 803rd Engineer Aviation Battalion.

Over here with his Camels and whiskey
and a car that wouldn't fit down some of our lanes,
cussing the narrow way we lived,

printing notes on the back Laying asphalt - break time - No. 12 Shoes -
(who else would catalogue an asphalt finisher's size?)
typing over the front Bridge to Argyll Castle - old as hell.

How he remembered our little island - farm, palace, castle,
henge, road, strip, lawn - an inventory of constructions
and the flower garden where he lived was just etc.

Imagine

Imagine waking up to sea, the warm silt of it
washing through your house, shivery deposits
jostling, nudging, settling between the carpets
and floorboards. In the kitchen is an ammonite

pulsing like a nautilus, tentacles and blow tube
hoovering through sunlit water past your fridge.
Urchins glide across the sofa. Two starfish edge
around the stairwell's flickering light bulb.

Your neighbour's cabbages are swimming off,
wobbling and bumping down Brize Norton Road.
His tomatoes are on the A40 and a shed load
of chickens is laying Size 2 eggs on your roof.

Everything's either sliding away or sinking.
Geese perch on the wings of stranded Tristars.
Cash machines spit bubbles. Buses and cars
end up on the runway, their hazards winking.

Nobody's shopping today, that's for sure.
Nobody's flying off to war. You've chucked
your mobile and VISA card and packed
enough groceries for a week or more.

You strike out one night under a full moon,
arms scything like windmill blades. A soldier
in a bathtub is singing through a loud hailer.
A Styrofoam tray bobs past, a plastic spoon.

Children paddle front doors while grandparents
sit on chairs and tell them stories. One by one
what kept us apart joins up - Persian, Aegean,
Caspian, Red, Baltic, North, Irish, Barents.